Playing Marbles with Diamonds

And Other Messages for America

Vance Havner

BAKER BOOK HOUSE
Grand Rapids, Michigan 49506

ISBN: 0-8010-4290-9

Printed in the United States of America

Contents

FOREWORD:
Vance Havner Reflects on Seventy Years of Ministry

Any desire that God puts in your heart, He wishes it to be filled," says Vance Havner. "All I've ever wanted to do was preach and write."

Vance Havner is said to have never known a time when he wasn't called to be a preacher. He made his peace with God at the age of ten years in the backwoods of Vale (Jugtown), North Carolina.

Licensed to preach at twelve and ordained at fifteen, he stood in a chair at First Baptist Church of Shelby,

North Carolina, and preached to a congregation of eigh-
teen hundred. It was an awesome experience for a boy
that young. And a great beginning.

" 'Boy preachers never last' is what they said," re-
flects Havner. "I've been preaching seventy years. I
would say, I've given it a pretty good try."

Who is this unique man of God? Evangelist Billy Graham calls him the most quoted preacher in America
today, and adds that no one in his generation has stirred
revival fires in the hearts of people across our nation
like Vance Havner has.

Havner calls himself "just a preacher." His warm and
witty personality, depth of insight, and simple, old-
fashioned preaching are refreshing. He stays free of (and
condemns) the red tape and formalities that stifle many
modern preachers. And while he doesn't claim to have
the answer for every problem, he holds to some old
truths that could cure a host of them.

During his seventy years in the ministry Havner has
remained uniquely himself. Though it is a different
world today than when he was called in 1924 to Salem
Baptist Church in Weeksville, North Carolina, Havner
comments, "Nothing of importance has changed."

While other ministers follow a more traditional route
of education, resulting in a Master of Divinity degree,
Havner should be honored with a B.W. (backwoods) degree. Although he attended Boiling Springs High School,
Wake Forest Baptist College, Catawba College, and
Moody Bible Institute, Havner never stayed anywhere
long enough to graduate.

"I'm not against education," Havner explains. "A person needs all he can get. But let every man follow his
own heart. I wanted to preach. Professor Huggins was
principal of Boiling Springs High School. He told me,

'My job is to get boys ready for Wake Forest College. But if I were you, I'd blaze my own trail.' And that's what I did."

In the spring of 1971 Havner preached the commencement sermon at Gardner-Webb College (formerly Boiling Springs High School) and was awarded an honorary degree of Doctor of Divinity from that institution. He was also nominated for the "Preacher of the Year" award in 1973 by *Decision* Magazine of the Billy Graham Evangelistic Association. These high honors prove Havner's saying, "You don't have to be included in 'Who's Who' to know what's what."

A wordsmith, Havner writes with the same wit, enthusiasm, power, and conviction that he uses in his preaching. On paper or in person, he gives the phrase "play on words" a new meaning, and keeps his listeners' attention with his homespun humor while delivering a convicting message that leaves an impression on their lives.

Why does Havner turn down more invitations at age 83 than three full-time evangelists could commit themselves to? Probably because he has a fresh word from God, uncontaminated with the desire to be famous, flattered, or filthy rich.

"Young preachers ask me how to get started in this business. I just started. I don't promote myself, hand out brochures, or have an organization. But of course God has put me in the right places at the right time and introduced me to some key men."

Unashamed and uninhibited, Havner preaches with power and boldness. "I take the bull by the horns when I preach," he explains. "I'm not trying to build a fan club or make a reputation for myself. I make my messages hard. God means business and we that preach should also. The gospel isn't cheap. It cost God his Son and the Son His life, and it'll cost us everything to follow Him. Jesus demands a lot from us, but He has a right to.

"I tell folks wherever I preach the devil's main business is to get people to join the church without being converted. I don't see many signs of revival in our country. There's not many excited about God in our churches today. I used to watch people at the depot in Maiden, North Carolina, as a boy. They nicknamed the old C&NW train, 'Can't and Never Will.' The train was old hat for a lot of people, but for those who were expecting a loved one to return, oh, boy! that was a different story. There were smiles on their faces and they were filled with excitement. The church should be expecting a loved one to return soon—Jesus Christ. But I don't see many excited about it. It seems that many preachers are more concerned with bringing in the kingdom than they are with bringing back the king. We'll not convert folks with bold slogans or show business. Preachers can't stir up revival on earth; revival has to fall like fire from heaven. The man that God uses to stir revival fires may not be from the same fabric that seminaries turn out these days. He may be a man uncultured and uneducated by the world's standards. It'd be refreshing to see a man with a well-worn Bible from the backwoods who has spent time with God."

Havner, who appears out-of-step with modern times, testifies that through the years he has made a habit of getting away from the hustle and bustle that consumes so much of our lives. He continues to bird watch as he did when a boy. He often takes to the back roads to meditate on the things of God, a fact that provides a clue as to where Havner's wisdom, practical applications, and preaching power come from.

"Meditation is a lost art among most preachers today," says Havner. "They're too busy, wrapped up with programs and committee meetings. We're not always doing the best thing when we're the busiest. If a preacher goes out 'walking' today he looks so suspicious the police are likely to arrest him, assuming he's sneaking around to steal something. I love God's woods. Some believe I should go back to the woods! But it's difficult to find a place to walk and meditate on the things of God today."

Reflecting on countless miles and seventy battle-worn years of serving God, Havner says, "It's been wonderful. God has blessed me so much. He has provided in every way. . . . What little I've done has been a result of God. I've often looked around and asked myself, 'How in the world did I get here?' God has often surprised me, putting me in wonderful situations I never dreamed of.

"God has blessed me with a writing ministry. The first little book I wrote in 1934, *By the Still Waters,* is still selling. The biggest seller I've had was *Though I Walk Through the Valley.* I wrote it after Sara, my wonderful wife, died in 1972. . . . We were married for thirty-some marvelous years. I loved her so much. . . . I've been discouraged and depressed, but nothing hurts like not having Sara.

"I hear from folks all over the country. They say, 'Your books are a blessing, especially, *Though I Walk Through the Valley.'* I never realized there were so many hurting, feeling similar to how I feel about Sara. It's all been a mystery to me. At times I wondered, where is God in all of this fog? But He's been guiding me when I didn't know where I was going. He has been with me all the way."

Vance Havner has "blazed his own trail." He has enjoyed the fulfillment of the desires of his heart. And even when men have misunderstood him because of his unorthodox compliance with the status quo, God has mightily used him to comfort, challenge, and convict, and to stir the fires of revival in local churches like no other preacher in the twentieth century. In his own words, "My ministry is to comfort the afflicted and to afflict the comfortable."

We who listen to his preaching, read his books, and meditate on his words for the seasoning of our souls love him and thank God for him. And we ask God for more grace as we so liberally use his sermon outlines, quote his clever one-liners, and pepper his illustrations throughout our sermons.

Like an old prophet who won't and can't be silenced, may he continue to burn with God's message and glow with His love. Then we shall continue to be inspired through this unique and remarkable man of God, Vance Havner.

Dennis Hester

1

Playing Marbles
with Diamonds

This is a day of depreciation and devaluation. Financiers have been worried about the French franc, the British pound, and the American dollar. But economics is not the only area that has been cheapened these days. We live in an age of sham and make-believe, superficiality and ballyhoo, lowered values, and marked-down prices.

America has been sold short. We despise our national birthright and make light of our heritage. It is time we rediscovered what it means to be an American, time we understood the price our fathers paid in blood, sweat, and tears to make this the land of the free and the home of the brave.

The nation is crumbling because our homes have been devalued; what was once a man's castle has become only a place in which to change clothes. Once man was the head of the home and woman the heart. Now we have two heads and no heart—and such a home is a monstrosity. Marriage has been reduced to a joke and is no longer a lifetime contract. We have cheap marriages and cheap homes because there are too many cheap people who lack the integrity to keep any contract.

Millions of Americans admired Mamie Eisenhower for showing old-fashioned grief at the funeral of the man who had been her sweetheart for over half a century. There was something about Ike and Mamie that put a lump in our throats and reminded us of those good old days when a bride and groom understood that marriage was for keeps. People used to weep at funerals and when they got converted; we could stand some of that today in this age that sees something admirable in being dry-eyed stoics ashamed to shed a tear.

We have never had so many high-priced clothes hung on so many low-priced people as we do today. Behind all our trouble is cheap character. My father was a poor man. He had few of this world's goods and when he visited the county seat town of my boyhood days he was no haberdasher's model. But he was an honest and respected man whose word was his bond and whose name was sufficient collateral to get money if he needed it. But today he would be considered a "square" because he never made his way through this world by shrewdness and trickery.

When I went off to boarding school as a country lad, I

remember that my roommate was a town boy. When he hung his high-priced neckties on his side of the dresser and I draped my cheap variety opposite I sensed the disparity and felt embarrassed. That went on for some days and then I came across some immortal words like these:

> What tho on homely fare we dine,
> Wear hodden gray and a' that,
> Give fools their silks and knaves their wine,
> A man's a man for a' that!
> For a' that and a' that,
> The honest man, tho' e'er so poor,
> Is king o' men for a' that!

Bobby Burns dispelled my shame and from that day to this no fool with his silks or knave with his wine has ever embarrassed me.

All of this cheapening that is going on has its roots in the spiritual. We are suffering today from a *cheap concept of God.* In the Book of Psalms we read: "Thou thoughtest that I was altogether such an one as thyself" (Ps. 50:21). It is the world that plants such ideas in our heads. The world tells us that God is just like us and that he is a grandfatherly being trotting His children on His knee and winking at the wickedness of the sons of men. All this silly talk about the "man upstairs" and the "big buddy," this slapping the Almighty on the back in rude and coarse familiarity, all these pitiful songs and ridiculous books that devalue Deity and bring a holy and righteous God down to our level, are but indexes to our spiritual poverty. Man has been defiled and God has been humanized. (One church-related college put on a musical skit in which God was portrayed in swimming trunks, perched on a ladder and engaging in profanity.)

A young woman in Vienna visiting the place where Beethoven's piano was on display had the audacity to sit down and play some rock-and-roll music on that rare instrument. The old caretaker remarked that Paderewski had once visited that spot. When the teenage tourist asked what he had played the old custodian replied, "Nothing. He felt unworthy to play Beethoven's piano!"

We have developed a generation incapable of reverence and worship in the presence of a holy God. Watch the average Sunday morning church congregation, how they come into church and how they go out, the listlessness of the listeners who "hearing, hear not." If the minister stopped half-way through his sermon and called on everybody to report what they were thinking about, the results would be astounding! There are other ways of taking God's name in vain than by using profanity. We do it when we sing songs and recite Scripture that has no meaning for us.

One reason for cheap worship nowadays is a cheap Bible. I am not preaching bibliolatry but the venerable old Book is now being devalued by critics who sit in judgment to determine what is inspired and what is not, making every man his own judge as to what he will accept as the Word of God. My Lord did not defeat the devil with His own power or wisdom but by quoting the Scriptures. The preacher needs to remember that what moves men's hearts is the Word of God, not our comments about it. We hear these days that everything depends on how you look at it. Rather, everything depends on how *God* looks at it and what *He* says about it.

Historian Edward Gibbon says that the Greek church fathers of the tenth century who handled the literature of early Christianity "held in their lifeless hands the riches of their fathers without inheriting the spirit which had created and improved that sacred patrimony. They read, they praised, they compiled but their languid souls seemed incapable of thought and action." So do men handle the Scriptures today and the living book of the dead becomes a dead book to the living.

Because we have a cheap concept of God and a cheap Bible, we have *cheap salvation.* Salvation is free but not cheap. We are not redeemed with silver and gold but with the blood of Jesus Who gave Himself a ransom for many. The writer of Hebrews speaks of those who count the blood of the covenant an unholy thing. One translation puts it, "who treats as a cheap thing"; another, "treated like dirt." There are those today who say they like Christ but not the church. But our Lord loved the church and gave Himself for it, purchased it with His blood. How can we love the head and not the body, the groom but not the bride?

We have a *cheap church* today because everybody is in it. Anybody can get in and nobody gets out. What started as a sheepfold looks more like a zoo! I am speaking of the professing church. The true church is a costly church, not in buildings and in earthly status but because it is the property of Christ bought with His blood. Men have devalued it but God hasn't!

A cheap church means *cheap Christians.* God's people are "a peculiar people" (1 Peter 2:9) which means "a purchased people." The Greek word here carries the idea of making a ring around something to mark it as one's own. Christ has made a ring around us and claimed us for Himself. We hear these days about "cheap grace" and how it doesn't mean much to be a Christian. But salvation is the costliest item on earth. It cost our Lord everything to provide it and it costs us everything to possess it. True, it is free but when one becomes a believer he also becomes a disciple and that costs him everything he has. Our Lord never put discipleship in fine print in the contract. He called on us to forsake all, take up our cross, deny self, love Him more than all else. We are not our own, we are bought with a price, the personal property of Jesus Christ with no right to anything. "Love so amazing, so divine, demands my soul, my life, my all."

> Naught that I have my own I call,
> I hold it for the Giver;
> My heart, my strength, my life, my all,
> Are His and His forever.

The Christian is to build his life with gold, silver, and precious stones—not wood, hay, and stubble. It costs to rear an edifice that will meet the fire-test of the last day. We are a generation of cheap Christians going to heaven as inexpensively as possible; religious hobos and spiritual deadbeats living on milk instead of meat, crusts of bread instead of manna, as though we were on a cut-rate excursion.

We are beset today by an epidemic of cheap religious music and gospel jazz. We have come from hymns to hootenannies. Somehow we have gotten the notion that we must drag the gospel down to the level of this age to make it please the perverted tastes of this generation. The natural man cannot receive spiritual truth and it is not only stupid but sinful to get folksy with Sodom and Gomorrah to make our message acceptable. The whole sickening business is the clever strategy of Satan to debase the holy into the profane. The gospel was never meant for entertainment nor was the church ever intended to play the accompaniment to the music of this world.

In a day when tragedy has become comedy, we play fast and loose with eternal issues. The pearl of great price is not cheap! I have read that years ago in that part of Africa where diamonds in the rough were plentiful, a traveler chanced on boys playing. Closer investigation revealed that they were playing marbles with diamonds! God forgive us today that we handle His treasures as though they were trifles and the coinage of the eternal as though it were play money. It is no time to play marbles with diamonds!

2

The Country and the Church

Recently I listened to a group of high school students being interviewed on television. They were asked what they thought about the situation in America today and they replied unhesitatingly that patriotism is almost extinct, that we have lost respect for the heritage of our past and the leadership of the present. It is the same as with Rome in her last days—same symptoms, same disease.

> Sad fares the land, to hastening ills a prey,
> Where wealth accumulates and men decay.

21

Once again history repeats itself and all that we learn from history is that we learn nothing from history.

There is a striking parallel today between conditions in our country and conditions in the church. When I speak of the church I do not mean the true church—God's remnant—which will neither decay nor die. I mean that vast ecclesiastical system, the professing church, Laodicea, "rich, and increased with goods, (needing) nothing" (Rev. 3:17).

Both America and the church have grown rich in what money can buy, but they are bankrupt in what money cannot buy. We can state with Peter Aquinas, "No longer can the church say 'Silver and gold have I none' but no longer can she say 'rise and walk.' " The church can stand anything else more than she can stand prosperity and popularity. She is poor when she is rich, secure in danger but endangered by security. She usually has most treasure in heaven when she has least on earth.

Our Lord would have the church be rich (Rev. 3:18)—not *get* rich but *be* rich—in all that she (the bride) has in Christ (the groom) Who "though He was rich for our sakes became poor that we through His poverty might be rich." Both in America and in the church, our problem is material plenty and spiritual poverty.

America has lost her regard for the flag. The Stars and Stripes have become cheap and commonplace, patched onto blue jeans, showing up just about anywhere without significance. Gone are the days when the flag brought tears to the eyes, a lump in the throat, a tug at the heart. Its white no longer means purity, its blue does not stand for loyalty, its red no longer represents the blood of martyrs who died that this flag might wave long o'er the land of the free and the home of the brave.

The banner of the church is the cross and God forbid that we should glory in anything else! But it is the cross of *Christ*, for a Christless cross is as meaningless as a crossless Christ. But the church has devised a new cross today: an ornament to wear around the neck, a commonplace symbol twisted out of context, a charm, a holy horseshoe. Such an ornament does not interfere with godless living, never goes against the grain of our old nature. On Sunday morning we sing,

> To the old rugged cross I will ever be true,
> Its shame and reproach gladly bear . . .

but we sing it totally unconscious of what it means to bear His reproach and, if we did know, totally unwilling to bear that cross any kind of way, let alone gladly.

It is about time the Stars and Stripes meant something again in America. It is about time the cross of Jesus Christ meant something again to the church. During the First World War the great tenor Enrico Caruso visited one of our great cities to give a concert. His last number was "The Star Spangled Banner" and when, with that matchless voice he reached the last word, he sang it an octave higher than written. When he finished, it was a long time before the audience could be quieted. I'd like to see a crowd of modern Americans get that excited today about Old Glory and I'd like to see a church full of professed Christians get happy some Sunday morning singing,

> In the cross of Christ I glory,
> Towering o'er the wrecks of time;
> All the light of sacred story
> Gathers round its head sublime.

The way we sing it now sounds more like a lullaby than a reveille!

As the Constitution of the United States means little to Americans today, so too the Bible means little to the average church member. Everybody has one; it lies in church pew racks; it gathers dust on tables. Fine things are said about it, lovely tributes are paid to it, but few there be who make it the rule of their life.

Church members generally are as ignorant of the Bible as are Americans of the Constitution. Now we are not called to bibliolatry. But the Bible is the only authorized textbook of our faith. Jesus said, "The words that I speak unto you, they are spirit and they are life." His words are recorded here and nowhere else. The Bible is God-breathed and when one explores this old book, he has the feeling, as Dr. J. B. Phillips puts it, of an electrician wiring an old building where the power has not been cut off: some get a charge and some get a shock but they discover that here is the only book in existence originally wired from heaven! In a day when the living faith of the dead has become the dead faith of the living, just as America needs to get back to the Constitution, so the church needs to return to the cross and the Bible.

America suffers from another problem. Too many people within our borders are Americans in name but are un-American in their hearts and anti-American in their conduct. The church has a corresponding ailment. Too many church members are Christians in name, but in reality are only once-born children of Adam. Theodore Roosevelt said during the First World War, "If you are an American and something else, you are not an American." He spoke of "hyphenated Americans" with a divided loyalty between this country and some other. The Scriptures say, "Whosoever will be a friend of the world is the enemy of God." Billy Sunday used to say of the worldly Christians, "You might as well talk about a heavenly devil." America will improve when we have better Americans and the church will improve when we have better Christians.

Author Gerald Johnson wrote: "What we need is not the flatterer who tells the American citizen what a wonderful fellow he is but what a wonderful thing it is to be an American. What we need is a challenger who will tell him what a difficult and dangerous thing it is to be an American for the American doctrine was devised by brave men for brave men." We ought to remember the price our forefathers paid in blood, sweat, and tears; that George Washington and his footsore soldiers did not stain the snow of Valley Forge with their blood just to create a politician's paradise; that Abe Lincoln did not walk the White House floor night after night to pass away the time. Every young American and every foreigner coming here to live ought to learn that it cost plenty to win this freedom and costs more to keep it. This is no time to despise our American birthright and make light of our heritage.

By the same token, when a man walks down the aisle to join a church, he ought to know what it means to be a Christian. We ought not flatter but rather challenge him. He ought to know that salvation is free but not cheap, that he is bought and paid for by the blood of Jesus Christ and that while Jesus paid it all, all to Christ he owes. The faith of our fathers has been preserved through dungeon, fire, and sword. When we cheapen and popularize it to make it acceptable to this world we insult God. Even the world has no respect for cheap Christians.

America suffers from a low-grade patriotism. Love for

our country and for her past heritage left to us by great men and women; enthusiasm for her rocks and rills, her woods and templed hills, is at a record low. During the First World War we fought with a sense of mission, to make the world safe for democracy (it hasn't been safe for anything since!). That patriotism grew weaker by the Second World War and almost disappeared in the Korean and Viet Nam Wars, which we were afraid to win and ashamed to lose. Today in a new internationalism we have lost our national integrity. We forget that a man is a better citizen of the world of nations when he is true to his own nation, a better member of the human family if he is a good member of his own family.

The church is a holy nation. Our citizenship is in heaven and there should be a spiritual patriotism, a love for the colony of heaven to which we belong if we are Christians, a love that transcends our affection for any earthly country. But just as America has gone international so the church has gone universal in the wrong way. Some professing Christians are so "universal" that they do not know how to be "local," so general that they cannot be particular, so excited about the world church that they are not worth much in a home church.

Certainly the church should not be isolated from the world but we must be insulated against a false togetherness that would destroy our distinctive testimony; we must be immunized against universalism.

There are those who say the church should take her place in the family of world religions and renounce her distinctive claim that there is no other name under heaven given among men whereby we must be saved. But we are called out of the world to go back into it and win others out of it—and that is our only business in it!

The American spirit is sadly eroded today by distrust,

by corruption in high places, by moral decay. It won't be restored merely by flag-wavings and drum-beatings and Fourth-of-July speeches. It may not be possible to raise a new crop of patriots in such shallow soil. It may take disaster to make us realize what we had. We may not miss the water until the well goes dry.

Just as there is an American spirit that sadly needs reviving, there is also a Christian spirit in the church that has that need. But it is not worked up by human excitement, religious enthusiasm of the flesh. It is the love of God shed abroad in our hearts by the Holy Spirit. It will magnify Jesus Christ for it is the business of the Holy Spirit to exalt our Lord.

Would to God that Americans might just be Americans and that Christians might just be Christians! But that will not be brought about simply by formal days of prayer put on by Chambers of Commerce, civic clubs, and carnal churches. When in the nation and in the church we humble ourselves, pray, seek God's face, and turn from our wicked ways, then God will hear from heaven, forgive our sin, and heal our land. I hear nothing coming out of Washington that sounds like that! We brag instead that Americans have licked every crisis in the past and that we can do it again. Such is the pride that goeth before destruction and the haughty spirit that precedes a fall. I don't hear much of this note in the church. Instead we boast of our denominational prestige and forget that God resists the proud and gives grace to the humble.

When the Titanic sank in 1912 the last music played by the ship's band as the great liner descended into icy waters was "Nearer, my God to Thee." It was a little late for that. Time is also running out on us today, both in the state and church.

"Sail on, sail on, O Ship of State!" Yes, but we had better pray while the ship is sailing and not wait until the ship is sinking! What time is it? "It is time for Thee, Lord, to work"—that is God's business. "It is time to seek the Lord"—that is our business. It is time in the country and in the church to make God's business our business!

3

God Never Comes Next

"Suffer me first. . . ." Luke 9:59
"Seek ye first. . . ." Matt. 6:33

Life is a matter of priorities. The quality of our living is determined by those things to which we give first place. With too many of us, the first has become last and the last first and our biggest business is to rearrange our priorities.

A certain man, invited by our Lord to become His disciple, said, "Suffer me first to go and bury my father." He was really saying, "My father is old and I must take care of him until he dies and then bury him. After that you will be next and I will follow you, but not now. Something else comes first." Our Lord replied in no uncertain terms, "Let the dead bury their own dead, you go and preach the kingdom of God!" He was saying in effect, "I do not come *next*. I come *first* or not at all. I do not play second fiddle."

Another prospective disciple said, "Lord, I will follow thee; but let me *first* go bid them farewell, which are home at my house." After the farewells, Jesus would come *next*. But our Lord sternly replied, "No man, having put his hand to the plow, and looking back, is fit for the kingdom of God." He was saying, "My kingdom is no place for a man with his face pointed one way and his feet the other. I am not taking people to heaven backwards."

Over against all this, our Lord said, "Seek ye *first* the kingdom of God and his righteousness; and all these things shall be added unto you." The temporal needs of life will be added, not subtracted. They have their place but not first place. There is a place for taking care of dear ones and if we do not so provide we are worse than infidels (1 Tim. 5:8). There is a time and a place for farewells. But Jesus Christ does not come *next* after all else has been attended to. He demands more allegiance than any dictator who ever lived—because He deserves it.

>Love so amazing, so divine,
>*Demands* my soul, my life, my all.

We sing, "Savior, *more than life* to me," "Jesus is *all the world* to me," "Thou from hence my *all* shalt be," "Now *Thee alone* I seek; give what is best." But we are usually at least partially unconscious when we sing in church. If we took stock of what we were singing, we might not be able to make it honestly through the first verse!

On one occasion when a great multitude went with Jesus, He must have thinned them out when He declared that we must hate loved ones and even our own lives, take our cross and forsake all we have to follow Him (Luke 9:24). Dr. A. T. Robertson explains that this is the language of exaggerated contrast, but we must not water it down until the point is gone. Our God is a jealous God and there must be no other gods before Him.

Throughout the Bible, marriage is a type of Jehovah's Old Testament relationship to His chosen people, Israel, and Christ's New Testament relationship to His purchased people, the church. The Scriptures are rigidly explicit, without exception or qualification, that when a man or woman contemplates marriage, the prospective mate must come first and take precedence over everything and everybody in this world. There are no extenuating circumstances that allow anything else. As the marriage ceremony puts it on the authority of Scripture (Matt. 19:5; 1 Cor. 11:3; Eph. 5:22–23), husband and wife must forsake all others and cleave only to each other until death do them part. This is not limited to its application to adultery in heart or act but to love for anyone or anything that takes priority over husband or wife. When anybody or anything comes first in our affections ahead of Jesus Christ, then He is not first—but He *never comes next*. When He does not hold the preeminence in our lives there is spiritual adultery, for if we are Christians we are married to Him (Rom. 7:4).

James wrote: "Ye adulterers and adulteresses, know ye not that the friendship of the world is enmity with

God? whosoever therefore will be a friend of the world is the enemy of God" (James 4:4). More than physical adultery is in mind in James's warning. Worldliness is spiritual adultery.

So, whether it be husband and wife in earthly relationships or "that happy bond that seals our vows to Him, our Savior and our God" in the heavenly relationship, one truth stands out as clear as day: what is first must be first. There is no earthly priority ahead of husband and wife, and our Lord will not share the throne of our hearts with another. He is not only First, He is Last, Alpha and Omega, and all the rest of the alphabet of our loves and concerns, earthly and heavenly, fit somewhere in between.

No man worth his salt would wait long on a woman who would reply to his proposal by saying, "I love you but there are other responsibilities and possibilities I must consider first. After that, you will be next." While she was attending to these other priorities he would find some prospect who had no priorities ahead of him! It is not a matter of wanting to be first on the totem pole, it is the way God ordained it. True love never puts the supreme object of that love second or next or last. Our Lord spoke to the prospective disciples in our text in a manner that seems almost harsh but He is asking, "Lovest thou me more than these, anything, everything, anybody, everybody?" He wants no disciples to whom He is merely a casual concern, a minor matter. When Abraham started to offer up Isaac, it proved that God came first and Isaac second. God took the will for the deed and spared Isaac, for it is as good as done when the heart is willing. The invited guests for the supper in one of our Lord's parables put land, oxen, and wife first. The rich farmer in another parable put prosperity first and

his soul second, but God said, "Thou fool, *this night* thy
soul shall be required of thee . . ." (Luke 12:20). It is not
a matter of "Suffer me first" but rather "Seek ye first."
He must have the preeminence, the precedence, the priority. Anything beside which He is second is an idol.

> The dearest idol I have known,
> Whate'er that idol be,
> Help me to tear it from its throne
> And worship only Thee.

We began by saying that life is a matter of priorities.
If you have a problem it may be that your priorities are
out of order somewhere. When Christ is alpha and
omega, first and last, all else falls into place. When He
is head of the home—not merely our guest but our
host—problems will be solved. When Christ and His
kingdom come first, when husband and wife put each
other first under the lordship of Christ, houses will
become homes.

When our Lord says "Follow me," let us forget funerals and farewells and stop saying, "Lord, I will follow
thee *but. . . .*" I am tired of all the talk about what we
must sacrifice to follow Jesus Christ. Look at what we
get! No man or woman thinks in terms of sacrifice to
get the mate they love. What country girl would hold
onto her trinkets if she could marry a prince!

> No mortal can with Him compare
> Among the sons of men;
> Fairer is He than all the fair
> Who fill the heavenly train.
> To Him I owe my life and breath
> And all the joys I have;
> He makes me triumph over death
> And saves me from the grave.

He deserves to be first and He demands it. He is not standing, hat in hand, like a bargain on an auction block waiting for some sinner to "accept" Him. Actually, the word is not "accept" but rather "receive, believe, trust, come, commit, follow." The real issue is, Will *He* accept *us*? Indeed He will for He said, "Him that cometh to me I will in no wise cast out." But while salvation is free it is not cheap. It cost God His Son and the Son His life. Jesus paid it *all* but *all* to Him we owe.

The other side of trusting Jesus as Savior is confessing Him as Lord, and that means making Him the all-inclusive priority in our lives—first and last. We do not wait until all the funerals and farewells have been attended to, until we have buried father and told the family goodbye, until we have built bigger barns, until some more opportune time, until we feel like it.

Too many church members sit smugly in church on Sunday, some closing the eyes and others eyeing the clothes, and with a dozen other things ahead of God in their lives. Some love a pet dog more than they love almighty God. They are saying, "Suffer me *first* ... to attend to a hundred other items before I get around to Jesus Christ." But Christ is saying, "Seek ye *first* the kingdom of God and His righteousness and *all these things* shall be added unto you." I am weary of begging proud sinners to come down church aisles and "take Jesus" as though they were doing Him a favor and the church an honor. We used to come saying,

> I am coming to the cross,
> I am poor and weak and blind;
> I am counting all but dross;
> I shall full salvation find.

All who come like that He will tenderly receive. But when we become believers we become also disciples and the terms for traveling that straight and narrow way are rigidly serious. Few there be that find it. There is no time to wait for funerals and farewells. Beware of the peril of the uncounted cost, the unburied corpse, and the unforsaken circle. Jesus Christ is the first and last, author and finisher, beginning and end, alpha and omega, and by Him all other things hold together. He must be first or nothing. God *never comes next!*

4

The Middle of the Book

It seems to be common practice to quote only part of Romans 8:28. Many people get no further than "All things work together for good." A few more add "to them that love God" and fewer still endure unto the end with "to them who are the called according to His purpose." The last word "purpose" wraps up the whole matter—for the blessed assurance promised here is only for the people of God's purpose. It is not for every Tom, Dick, and Harry with a sentimental micawberish philosophy that "everything will turn out all right anyway." God had something definite in mind from the beginning and if we understood better His objective from the start we would know better how to get with it and live within it. Too often God is out to do one thing and we are up to something else. When we become part of His purpose and love Him, then all things, including things not even good in themselves, can be made to contribute to the fulfillment of that purpose.

The Purpose of God is a book with three chapters. The first chapter began with creation and extends to the fall of man in the Garden of Eden. The second begins after the fall and continues until the return of Jesus Christ. The third begins with His coming again and never ends through all eternity.

We are living in the second chapter and sometimes it seems as though that chapter will never end. But one thing we *must* understand with perfect certainty: the middle of the book is no place from which to judge the whole book. Most of our confusion arises from trying to sum up the whole of God's purpose when we are only in the middle of the drama. The second chapter is neither the time nor the place to arrive at conclusions. Much of it makes no sense now but that does not mean that it never will make sense; because it makes no sense to us does not mean that it does not make sense to God.

These three chapters may be titled "The Original Purpose of God," "The Present Purpose of God," and "The Ultimate Purpose of God." The Bible does not begin with an argument to prove the existence of God. It begins rather with an affirmation: "In the beginning God"—and that is where *we* must begin. Neither does the Bible explain how evil started; it presents the serpent in the Garden of Eden. We need not waste our time trying to reason out the existence of God or the origin of evil; we need to accept them as facts and move on from there. God does not tell us all we might like to know but He tells us all we *need* to know for the outworking of His purpose.

The first chapter, "The Original Purpose of God," begins with God creating everything in an ideal state and the human race starting out in innocence. We can only imagine what things would be like today if that state had continued, but we know we would be living in a world without sin, sickness, disease, and death—in some respects like angels. That is not the way it turned out, however, for Adam and Eve ate us out of house and home. We lost Paradise and God's original purpose was temporarily spoiled by sin.

Why didn't God keep us in a state of innocence? Because He chose to give us the power of choice. But what a fearful responsibility came with that power! We could choose evil—and for centuries the world has wallowed in agony and grief, sorrow and shame—but we could also choose good. We had to have the power to choose either if we were to be free agents.

But Adam and Eve could not stay in Eden after they had sinned. God's original purpose having been disrupted, He began the second chapter, His "Present Purpose," revealed through His chosen people, Israel. His plan of redemption culminated in the coming of His Son to earth to save us from our sins. Some say that this was not our Lord's original intention, that He came to start a movement, to recruit disciples, and that His death on the cross was a secondary development. But the sacrifices and prophecies of the Old Testament point to Calvary, and to the Son of God becoming our sin. Left to our own devices, we would try to mop the floor and leave the faucet running, sweep away the cobwebs and do nothing about the spider. Sin is the cause of all our trouble and Jesus came to deal with sin; He came to reconcile us to God and bring us into the path of God's "Ultimate Purpose" (Chapter Three).

Today God is taking out from the world a purchased people for His name. One day our Lord will return and the saints will reign with Him over a redeemed creation. That creation is standing "on tiptoe," as Dr. J. B. Phillips puts it, waiting for that day of the manifestation of the sons of God, the restoration and regeneration and restitution of all things when the meek shall inherit the earth and take over. Man in his natural state is trying to build a new Paradise on earth by means of science and technology but he is doomed to failure. God is gathering out His people that they might be conformed to the image of His Son, the first Adam of that new race of the children of God. This is the process by which he carries out His purpose with his people.

That process has not been completed yet and we are in the middle chapter. We live in a world wrecked by sin and we Christians are still in our human bodies and the old Adamic nature has not been eradicated. We suffer like everybody else from the disease, accidents, and disappointments to which all men are heirs. But when troubles pile up and unanswered questions multiply, when right seems forever on the scaffold and wrong forever on the throne, when it seems that the Great Avenger is careless and looking the other way, we *must* not forget that we are in Chapter Two of the *Book of God's Purpose*. Heeding the advice of Paul to "judge nothing before the time, until the Lord come" (1 Cor. 4:5) we must not try to make final conclusions in the middle of the book.

In this chapter, the devil is on a long chain with a seemingly wide range, but God holds the other end of that chain. God makes some things happen and lets some things happen, but nothing ever "just happens." Everything that happens is in the book of His purpose and we cannot make sense out of some of it, but remember—this is the middle chapter!

We must never forget that things as they now are were not in the original purpose of God, nor are they in His ultimate purpose. Famine, pestilence, wars, and bad weather were not on the first blueprints, and they are not on the last. But in God's present purpose all these things can work together for good to His people, the people of His purpose as they consent to and cooperate with the process by which He works out that purpose in their lives. We make our way through grief and disaster, through unexplainable mysteries and through "whys" to which we see no answer, but the eternal purpose of God moves on. David may fall into sin, Peter may deny His Lord, and Christians may die under strange circumstances, but the purpose of God moves on. Our own little wave may seem to be defeated but of one thing we are sure, the tide will win! And that tide is the will of God, original, present, and future.

5

Look Who's Here!

When someone shows up unexpectedly, or when we suddenly encounter someone we have wanted to see or have not seen in a long time, we sometimes say, "Look who's here!" That expression could have been used often in the Bible. Think of the Israelites in the wilderness, often tempted to despair and even to rebel. But on many a night a Hebrew could pull back the flap of his tent, see the pillar of fire in the sky, and say to his companion, "Everything's all right. We're not alone. *Look who's here!*"

Or think of Elisha, the prophet of God and a one-man

Central Intelligence System. When the Syrian king planned a move against Israel, Elisha learned about it through his hot line to heaven. The king sent horses, chariots, and a great host of soldiers to capture this troublesome prophet. When Elisha's servant started out next day he saw the soldiers everywhere and, overwhelmed, cried to his master, "(What) shall we do?" Elisha replied, "Fear not: for they that be with us are more than they that be with them." The servant must have thought, "But I don't see them!" Elisha prayed that God might open his servant's eyes and when He did, the servant saw that "the mountain was full of horses and chariots of fire round about Elisha" (2 Kings 5:17). *Look who's here!* "The angel of the Lord encampeth round about them that fear him, and delivereth them" (Psalm 34:7). We need to raise our sights these days to see who is on our side. We cannot be optimistic with a misty optic!

Then there was Isaiah who had a vision of God the same year that King Uzziah died. King Uzziah's passing was a national calamity. His death under sad circumstances overwhelmed the nation. People were saying, "If a good man like our king can end up like that, what hope is there for the rest of us?" Isaiah, too, was stunned, but for him there was a plus along with the minus. "In the year that king Uzziah died, I saw *also* the Lord. . ." (Isa. 6:1). While everybody else saw disaster and despair, Isaiah saw the Lord, high and lifted up. Minus Uzziah but plus the Lord! *Look who's here!*

Do you remember the three Hebrew children in the fiery furnace? King Nebuchadnezzar looked in and said, "What's going on here? We threw three men into the furnace and I see four!" The three Hebrews might well have said, "We have company. *Look who's here!*" And they came out without even the smell of the smoke! The fourth in the fire made the difference!

Consider Daniel in the lions' den. King Darius was a mighty ruler but he couldn't sleep. He lived in a palace but he couldn't sleep. His bed was covered with costly tapestries but he couldn't sleep. He arose early next morning and went, bleary-eyed, down to the lions' den to ask Daniel, "How are you doing?" The prophet might well have answered, "You might as well have had your sleep. God sent his angel. *Look who's here!*"

John the Baptist stood at the Jordan and said to his listeners, "There standeth one among you whom ye know not," and the next day he declared, "Behold the Lamb of God!" Every Sunday morning there stands among the churchgoers one whom many of them know not. It is the business of the preacher to present the Christ who is always there when we meet in His name and bid the congregation, *"Look who's here!"*

Jesus stopped at Jacob's well one day and began to talk to a wicked woman. He spoke to her of the Water of Life but she said, "Thou hast nothing to draw with and the well is deep." She was correct in her facts but wrong in her conclusion. What difference does it make if the well is deep and there is nothing to draw with when one is in the presence of Jesus Christ! *Look who's here!*

At the house of Jairus, Jesus stated that the daughter was not dead, but only asleep. "And they laughed him to scorn *knowing that she was dead.*" They were correct in their facts but wrong in their conclusion. That is as far as atheism, agnosticism, and unbelief ever get. "She is dead and that settles it." When you're dead, you're dead! They had already sent word to Jairus before he reached his home. "Thy daughter is dead, why trouble the Master any further?" It was all over, nothing could be done. But when Jesus is present, death does not have the last word. When He is here, all considerations of mortal men fall short. *Look who's here!*

It is the same old argument of the scoffers Peter writes about who say, "Where is the promise of His coming? All things continue as they were from the beginning of the creation." In other words, there is nothing but natural law, cause and effect. Don't look for miracles. God is nowhere. But the Christian cuts that "nowhere" in two and says, God is *now here!*

But this very sense of God among us now, Jesus gathering where we meet in His name, the Holy Spirit consciously present, this is what we mean when we sing, "There's a sweet, sweet Spirit in this place." And the tragedy of our church life is that we produce everything else—and the occasional exception sadly reminds us of what should be the rule. How many church meetings have you attended that could be described best by saying, *God was here!*

At Bethany Martha said, "I know my brother will rise in the resurrection at the last day." She was right in her facts but wrong in her conclusion. She was a good fundamentalist but she didn't have to wait until the resurrection to see Lazarus live again. In front of her stood the Resurrection and the Life. *Look who was there!*

When Jesus said, "Roll away the stone from the sepulcher," Martha objected that Lazarus had been dead for four days and there would be a foul odor. She was right in her facts, wrong in her conclusion. What difference did it make if Jesus Christ was present? All other considerations don't matter in the face of that! *Look who's here!*

Our Lord was taking a nap in a boat on the Sea of

Galilee. A storm arose and the frantic disciples aroused Him, crying, "Carest Thou not that we perish?" They forgot that the *Son of God was there* in the boat with them. God gave Adam dominion over the birds of the air, the beasts of the earth, and the fish of the sea, but not over the wind and the waves. But when Jesus stood and said, "Be still!" that storm subsided and the amazed disciples said, "What manner of man is this that even the winds and the sea obey him!" He had what Adam never had—He is the new Adam! So the Christian can stand in any storm and say, *"So what! Look who's here!"*

After the resurrection our Lord stood on the shore of Tiberias. The disciples, who had fished in vain all night, did not recognize Him. He said, "Cast your net on the right side" and when they did they gathered more fish than they were able to haul in. John said to Peter, "It is the Lord!" *Look who's here!*

The Emmaus disciples were trudging along homeward from Jerusalem. They were bemoaning the fact that it was the third day since Calvary. That was exactly the reason why they should have gone down the road with one foot saying "Amen" and the other "Hallelujah!" because He had said He would rise on that day and they might meet Him at any turn of the road! They were right about it being the third day but wrong in their conclusion. One feels like saying to them, "It *is* the third day and look who is walking beside you. *Look who's here!"*

But we live in glass houses and cannot throw stones. Our Lord has said that where two or three gather in His name, He is there. What would happen if the average prayer meeting at church should ever take that seriously and believe it? Instead, we pray, "Lord, be with us" when He is already with us! Instead, we ought to shout, *"Look who's here!"*

Evan Roberts, God's spokesman in the Welsh revival, was fearful that the people might look to him instead of to the Lord. On one occasion he arrived late to where a throng had been waiting, as though he had to be present before anything much could happen. He asked the crowd, "Do you believe God is here as He promised when we gather in His name?" They shouted their agreement whereupon he put on his hat and coat and left! It was a dramatic way of saying that what matters is the presence of the Lord. In that great revival they had no advance publicity, no choirs, no song books, no order of service or offerings, no famous preacher (great preachers attended but they sat in the congregation). All they had in this revival was God. Maybe we'll get around to that some day again. Maybe sometime heaven will come down without our "packing the pew," pin-the-tail-on-the-donkey, talking horses, karate experts, and theatrical personalities. "Where my people gather in my name, there am I . . ."—that is not just a promise but a fact! It shouts, *"Look who's here!"*

What would happen if just for once we gathered believing that we were to experience the personal appearance of Jesus Christ? I have often been appalled by the careless and sometimes frivolous way church choirs often enter the sanctuary; they might as well be singing "Mary Had a Little Lamb." I have observed congregations that appear cold and casual, some more interested in who's wearing what than in the main event. And I have often been convicted in my own heart of the careless way I have sometimes entered the pulpit—taking for granted the fact that I am about to participate in the greatest kind of gathering possible to man. One should enter the pulpit as though it were the first time, as though it could be the best time, and as though it might be the last time!

God forgive us for gathering in His name, not expecting much to happen, praying for rain but not carrying our umbrellas. We pay church staffs to do church work and then assemble on Sunday to watch them do it! It is a performance, not an experience. When the preacher stands up to preach, the attitude is "All right, preacher, let's see what you've got." When he finishes we say in effect, "I move we accept this as information and be dismissed." No wonder we meet at eleven o'clock sharp and end at twelve o'clock dull.

In this day of standardized, systemized, and computerized business we Americans have become so proficient and efficient in our church work that we have only a small place left on the program for the supernatural and the miraculous. We seem not to need the Holy Spirit. We quote, "Not by might nor by power but by Thy Spirit," and sing, "Kindle a flame of sacred love in these cold hearts of ours," but like the Laodiceans, we are rich and increased with goods and have need of nothing. We are doing so well with our know-how, our expertise, that the good has become the enemy of the best and we are less and less open to divine invasion and intervention. We do not pray, "O that Thou wouldest rend the heavens and come down." We have little use for miracles. We begin to disbelieve them, even in the Bible. As a result, in our churches it is business as usual because we have no unusual business! We are doing much that could be done just as well in the civic club, the fraternal order, the political party. Ephesus may be sound in doctrine but has left her first love. Sardis may have a "name to be alive" but is dead (Rev. 3:1).

How are we going to regain that consciousness of God that makes the difference and is the evidence that we

are the people of God who Moses prayed about long ago
(Exod. 33:12–17)? Elijah demonstrated just that on
Mount Carmel. He called for a confrontation—a confrontation must always precede divine visitation; he re-
paired the altar and prepared the sacrifice—it is useless
to expect fire from heaven with an unprepared altar and
an unprepared sacrifice; then he did something that has
been given little attention—he poured twelve barrels of
water on the sacrifice. There had been a three-year
drought and water was the scarcest of commodities but
Elijah poured out what was most precious to make it
clear that if fire fell it must be from heaven. Today we
try to warm up the altar as if to help matters and make
it easier for God. It is the drenched altar that God sets
on fire. When we are prepared to be called fools if nothing happens and venture everything in holy desperation
the fire will fall and men will have to say, "The Lord,
He is God. *Look who's here!*"

Our Lord has promised to be with us when we gather
in His name (Matt. 18:20) and when we go with His
gospel (Matt. 28:19–20). But some say, "I can't see
Him." He said to Thomas, "Blessed are those who have
not seen and yet have believed." Peter was there when
he said it and later he wrote in his epistle, "Whom,
having not seen ye love; in whom, though now ye see
Him not, yet believing, ye rejoice with joy unspeakable
and full of glory." It is that faith that shouts to this
unbelieving world, *"Look who's here!"*

And one of these days, every eye shall see Him and all
who are ready for that great day will go marching home,
their troubles over, their questions answered, and their
tears wiped away, caught up to meet the coming King.
And it can all be summed up then in one mighty shout:
"Look who's here!"

6

Thorns

The Bible has much to say about thorns and thistles, briers and brambles. A score of different words are used to name them and around two hundred varieties of prickly shrubs grew in Bible countries. We have plenty of them in America as well. We have been scratched and irritated, lacerated and torn, and we have wondered why such pesky pests were created. Thorns and thistles are symbols of troubles, trials, and testings and some of us have so much of such adversity that we feel we could identify with Br'er Rabbit who was "born and bred in a brier patch."

The Scriptures throw much light on this subject;

learning the significance of thorns and thistles will help
us to understand the prickly problems of our own existence, and will help us make our way through the briers
and brambles of our troubled lives.

The Thorns of Creation

It begins with the *thorns of creation.* In the beginning
God put Adam and Eve in Eden where every prospect
was pleasing and not even man was vile. But the devil
came, followed by the fall, and God said to Adam:
"Cursed is the ground for thy sake; in sorrow shalt thou
eat of it all the days of thy life; *thorns also and thistles*
shall it bring forth to thee; and thou shalt eat the herb of
the field; in the sweat of thy face shalt thou eat bread,
till thou return unto the ground; for out of it thou wast
taken; for dust thou art, and unto dust shalt thou return" (Gen. 3:17–19).

We are still under that sentence and the more we try
to escape, the more we become entangled with thorns
and thistles—physically, morally, spiritually. The evo-
lutionist thinks we are working our way upward
through fetishism, totemism, polytheism, and mono-
theism to the knowledge of God but the Scriptures tell
us that we started with a knowledge of God and have
been going the other way ever since, not in evolution
but in "devilution."

The Thorns of Canaan

After the fall of man, God began a plan of redemption
for mankind and the whole creation. He called out the
Hebrew nation to be the channel through which the

Savior would come. He led them into the Promised Land and when they had conquered much of it and were beginning to settle in, He warned them, "But if ye will not drive out the inhabitants of the land from before you; then it shall come to pass, that those which ye let remain of them shall be pricks in your eyes, and *thorns* in your sides, and shall vex you in the land wherein ye dwell" (Num. 33:55). Joshua warned them that if they married among the Canaanites, those people would be "snares and traps and scourges in your sides and *thorns* in your eyes."

These *thorns of Canaan* must still be dealt with. Christians today, like the Hebrews of old, are a chosen generation, a holy nation. As God's people, He wants us to be separate, not to merge into the world around us, not to squeeze into its mold. "If any man love the world," said Jesus, "the love of the Father is not in him." Since Christianity began, there has never been a world culture in which a Christian can feel at home.

There can be no peaceful coexistence, no détente, between the Christian and Canaan. The friend of the world is the enemy of God. If we mix and mingle with this age it will soil and spoil our lives and ruin our testimony. The Christian lives not in collusion but in collision with this world.

Christians should not marry unbelievers. What looks innocent enough at the outset becomes a thorn in our side. A woman wearing a white dress wanted to explore a coal mine. When told that she was not properly garbed for such a trip, she demanded, "What's to keep me from wearing a white dress into a mine?" The man at the entrance replied, "There's nothing to keep you from wearing a white dress *into* the mine, but plenty to keep you from wearing a white dress *out!*"

Separation from the world is almost unheard-of

nowadays because this permissive and tolerant generation frowns on it. But we must beware of the thorns of
Canaan. "Canaanism" is dangerous, whether you call it
"worldliness," "secularism," or some other name, and
we are to have no fellowship with the unfruitful works
of darkness but rather expose them, not only by reproof
but by the contrast of godly living.

The Thorns of the Christian

Perhaps you have already anticipated what type of
thorn comes next. Many Christians and non-Christians
alike are familiar with Paul's "thorn in the flesh."
What was it? We do not know, and I am glad we do
not, for it might have been the same as your thorn or
the same as mine. Some think it was eye trouble. Anyway, it was an affliction that God would not remove.
This great preacher, this prisoner who set others free,
was not healed of whatever plague or infirmity beset
him all his days.

Notice that Paul calls his problem not only a "thorn
in the flesh" but also "the messenger of Satan" (2 Cor.
12:7). Paul gave the credit where it was due. He gloried
in his infirmity but he did not glorify his infirmity. Jesus had spoken of "this woman *whom Satan hath
bound*" and Paul wrote to the Thessalonians that he
was prevented from visiting them not because he was
"providentially detained" (as we preachers like to put it)
but because "Satan hindered me." Sickness, disease,
death, and all other thorns are of the devil but may be
allowed by God to test and try us and to glorify
Himself—as He made clear in the cases of Lazarus and
Peter. God may sharpen His axe on Satan's grindstone

(it cannot be done on a cake of butter!). Some of the greatest saints have made their way through this world with afflicted bodies, tortured minds, financial distress, domestic difficulties, and tragic circumstances; our pet answers and clever cliches provided no explanation, nor did prayer remove the thorn.

In the twelfth chapter of Second Corinthians Paul goes from height to depth, from his trip to the third heaven to his thorn in the flesh, observing that life's supreme experience is not in height or depth but in knowing that God's grace is sufficient, that His strength is made perfect in weakness, that when we are weak we are strong. It is worth a thorn in the flesh to learn that— and that is the way we usually learn it! It is when endurance flags and strength fails and resources play out that "from His infinite riches in Jesus God giveth and giveth and giveth again."

The Thorns of Christ

The thorns of creation, the thorns of Canaan, the thorns of the Christian . . . is there deliverance from all these? Yes, and it is signified by the *thorns of Christ,* that gruesome crown the Roman soldiers jammed on Jesus' already bruised and battered head. They did not realize what it symbolized any more than they understood his prayer, "Father, forgive them for they know not what they do." That ghastly diadem was emblematic of all the thorns of all time, a thorny creation ruined by sin, a thorny evil society like the Canaanites, all thorns of the flesh that torment the people of God. All the sin, all the suffering, all the disease, death, and heartbreak of all mankind was laid on Him.

> See from His head, His hands, His feet,
> Sorrow and love flow mingled down;
> Did e'er such love and sorrow meet,
> Or *thorns* compose so rich a crown?

One day that Christ who wore the crown of thorns will return to wear the crown of triumph. The creation will be redeemed and its original beauty restored, for God is not going to let the devil get away with the havoc he has wrought. No longer will an evil society like the Canaanites inhabit the earth, for the meek shall inherit it and the saints shall reign over it and for the first time law and order shall prevail. The thorns of all Christians will no longer exist, for the people of God will wear their new Easter outfits—their resurrection bodies—free from pain. And "instead of the thorn shall come up the fir tree, and instead of the brier shall come up the myrtle tree: and it shall be to the Lord for a name, for an everlasting sign that shall not be cut off" (Isa. 55:13).

Does Jesus care? That is why He came to this earth—to deal with the thorns of creation, the thorns of Canaan, and the thorns of the Christian, all gathered up in the thorns of Christ. It is time we sing not only with our lips but from our hearts,

> King of my life, I crown Thee now,
> Thine shall the glory be,
> Lest I forget Thy *thorn-crowned* brow,
> Lead me to Calvary.

7

Discernment

We are witnessing today the almost complete sellout of the professing church to this pagan world. That this is to be expected in the last days of this age as we draw near Babylon and the Antichrist does not excuse such a sellout, however; what is most appalling is that most major churchmen do not seem alarmed. One hears no note of protest, and religious leaders climb on every bandwagon without knowing which way the parade is headed. Well-meaning but weak-kneed Jehoshaphats are inveigled by modern Ahabs into joining all sorts of expeditions against Ramoth-gilead (1 Kings

22). Four hundred prophets urge them on and any Micaiah who dares to be "Prophet Number 401" is viewed as a hopeless reactionary out of step with the times.

Discerning the Truth

We cannot believe that all these confederates of Ahab mean to be quislings. The most charitable thing we can say is that they have no vision and cannot see through the fog. They lack *discernment,* and discernment is just about the scarcest commodity in the church today. Yet the Scriptures give it high priority. To begin with, we read: "But the natural man receiveth not the things of the Spirit of God: for they are foolishness unto him: neither can he know them, because they are spiritually *discerned*" (1 Cor. 2:14).

This simply means that the sons of Adam, no matter how high their intellectual and moral qualifications, cannot comprehend spiritual truth. One might as well describe a sunset to a blind man or music to a deaf man as to talk about the deep things of God to a man who has never been born again. What the man needs is sight, and spiritual sight comes only through the miracle of the new birth.

It is so difficult for us pompous Americans, so proud of our learning, to believe that the most common day laborer may apprehend divine truth while the literati may utterly miss it. The latter may be brilliant at discerning good poetry or chemical solutions; he may be able to solve problems in big business or locate bugs in engineering—but such ability is of absolutely no value in comprehending the things of God.

We cannot understand the Scriptures or gospel truth

in any form without spiritual discernment. A keen mind
and theological training are useful tools when they are
sanctified but the Holy Spirit is our teacher and He who
inspired the Bible is the best interpreter of it. How many
times have we heard a humble preacher with a limited
library preach nuggets of truth and gospel gems while
some scholar missed the truth completely? Now if the
little preacher had the scholar's library and the scholar
had the little preacher's discernment, we'd really be in
business! Blessed is the preacher who has both!

Discernment is as important in hearing the truth as in
preaching it. *How* we hear means as much as *what* we
hear. Some dear souls listen for years to sound preaching
and then, when a new preacher comes along preaching
error, they listen with equal satisfaction. So long as the
minister makes nice references to Jesus, these listeners
know no difference. They have no discernment. There is
a preparation *for* the sermon as well as a preparation *of*
the sermon. We are told to lay apart all filthiness and
superfluity of naughtiness and receive with meekness
the implanted word which is able to save our souls.
Everybody expects the preacher to be ready to preach
but who thinks of the congregation's responsibility to be
ready to listen?

Discerning the Times

Not only must we discern the truth, we must discern
the times. "Ye can discern the face of the sky; but can
ye not discern the signs of the times?" (Matt. 16:3). Like
the children of Issachar we need to understand the times
to know what Israel ought to do. "And that, knowing
the time, that now it is high time to awake out of sleep:

for now is our salvation nearer than when we believed"
(Rom. 13:11). A farmer, awakened in the night when his
clock went berserk and struck seventeen, rushed all
over the house waking everybody up and shouting, "It's
later than it ever has been before!" It *is* later than we
think and there is no other possible explanation for
these frightening times than the New Testament description of the last days before our Lord returns. True,
we have had famine and pestilence and earthquakes and
wars and rumors of wars from the beginning but never
with such frequency and intensity as now. Anarchy in
the world, apostasy in the professing church, apathy in
the true church, the emergence of Israel, the growing
world church, the approach of the Antichrist—one
would have to be blind in both eyes and bereft of his
brains not to see the hand of God assembling the pieces
of the world puzzle after the New Testament pattern. It
is about time we checked with God's clock. Peter tells
us that the scoffers will make light of this whole matter
and the man who sees no sign of our Lord's return is a
sign himself!

I remember spending an afternoon all alone on the
Mount of Olives. I found myself saying, "Lord, I don't
know when you are coming back but if it should be
today I'm at the right place to join the welcome committee. I'm standing where you will stand. "Even so,
come, Lord Jesus!"

Discerning the Spirits

There is another type of discernment that follows
logically after discerning the times. It is the discerning
of spirits. This is a special gift (1 Cor. 12:10) but we

also read, "Beloved, believe not every spirit, but try the spirits whether they are of God: because many false prophets are gone out into the world" (1 John 4:1). The man who can discern the truth and the times is also prepared to try the spirits.

Our Lord declared that false prophets and false Christs would arise, deceiving many. We are living in the worst period of deception in history. Satan is the master deceiver, disguised as an angel of Light. He specializes in simulation. The sin against the Holy Spirit was attributing the work of God to the devil. We are seeing today the work of the devil attributed to God. (I am more afraid of false revival than of no revival—a false revival with a false gospel, false evangelists, false converts, false joy. It will seem so genuine that it would deceive, if possible, the very elect. Many church leaders will endorse it. Other good people will be afraid to oppose it for fear that they might be fighting against God.)

What is the secret of discerning the spirits? How are we to know whether the spirits are from God? First, let us ask God for wisdom (James 1:5). He has promised to give it if we ask in faith, without wavering. Let us follow the guidelines of First John 4:2–3 immediately following the injunction to try the spirits: "Hereby know ye the Spirit of God: Every spirit that confesseth that Jesus Christ is come in the flesh is of God: And every spirit that confesseth not that Jesus Christ is come in the flesh is not of God: and this is that spirit of antichrist, whereof ye have heard that it should come; and even now already is in the world." Then let us remember our Lord's words: "My sheep hear my voice, and I know them, and they follow me" (John 10:17); "and a stranger will they not follow, but will flee from him: for they know not the voice of strangers" (John 10:5).

Riding through Israel I watched shepherds keeping flocks. Sometimes one shepherd kept several flocks. When the time came to separate them, his own sheep came to him because he had a peculiar whistle and they recognized that whistle. The best antidote against the counterfeit is a double dose of the genuine. The best way to detect counterfeit money is by knowing true currency so well that one can easily spot the false. The best way to discern the spirits is to be intimately acquainted with Jesus Christ. When the sheep know the shepherd's voice, they will not be deceived by the voice of strangers. We waste time studying false spirits when we might be getting better acquainted with the Holy Spirit.

Discerning the Lord's Body

There is another form of discernment that has never had the attention it deserves. We read about it in First Corinthians 11 where Paul writes about the observance of the Lord's Supper. He says that whoever partakes unworthily—in an unworthy manner, that is—is guilty of the body and blood of the Lord and eats and drinks judgment to himself, not *discerning* the Lord's body. We are further told, "For this cause many are weak and sickly among you, and many sleep" (1 Cor 11:30).

In the light of this, most of our Sunday morning church members are eligible either for the hospital or the graveyard! When we notice the careless way we rush through this ordinance tacked onto the end of a morning service, we marvel that we survive! The Lord's Supper is a memorial: we remember His death for us until He comes for us. To partake worthily is to come with proper regard for what He wrought for us on the cross. We are not ready to partake until we have examined ourselves, searched our hearts, *discerned* ourselves.

There is plenty of self-justification these days but not much self-judgment. I know of no better place for a revival to begin than at the Lord's Table. Revival begins when we stop justifying ourselves and begin judging ourselves. Proper discerning at the Lord's Supper begins with proper discernment of ourselves. Not only are we inviting the judgment of God when we hurry through this ordinance, we are missing a great opportunity for refreshment and revival.

But the Lord's Supper not only looks back to His death and forward to His coming, it has significance for us *now*. Christ is the Bread of Life, our meat and drink. As we partake of the Lord's Supper we are reminded that Christ is not only our Savior but also our Sustenance. I am a Baptist and sometimes I think that we Baptists, in our reaction against sacramentarianism, have gone so far the other way that we make too little of the Memorial Supper. We do well to remind ourselves at the Lord's Supper that we are declaring, among other things, that Christ is our food and drink and that we live by the conscious appropriation of the living Christ for every need. Here again a revival could begin if for once people discerned all that they have in Christ and laid hold on it.

Discerning Good and Evil

In the fifth chapter of Hebrews, the author writes about spiritual babes who have never grown up and are still on milk instead of meat. We are oversupplied with these adult babies in our churches. If we graded our members according to their spiritual development, many if not most of our fellowships would be in the beginners department! Christians grow like children grow—by food, rest, and exercise. When they do not feed on the Word, rest in the Lord, and exercise themselves unto godliness, they simply do not grow.

The writer of Hebrews says that Christians who are on milk instead of meat are "unskillful in the word of righteousness" but that "strong meat belongeth to them that are of full age, even those who by reason of use have their senses *exercised to discern both good and evil*" (5:14). A newer translation puts it "Their perceptions are trained by long use to discriminate between good and evil."

This does not mean that we try everything, good and bad, and out of that experience make up our minds as to which is which. Yet that is the position taken by much of modern youth as well as by their elders. Let any discerning Christian object to a filthy show or a vile book, for instance, and they will hear, "Have you seen the show? Have you read the book?" One need not drink liquor in order to decide whether it is right or wrong. Must one be an adulterer to make up his mind for or against immorality? We need not live in a hog pen and drink swill in order to form some idea of hogs. This pernicious and silly nonsense is the chatter of the undiscriminating who have not exercised their senses to discern good and evil.

How do we discern between good and evil? By using our faculties under the Holy Spirit, by prayer and the Word, and by sanctified common sense, making decisions as to what is right and what is wrong. Most of our church membership today is an untrained, undisciplined, mixed multitude with no knowledge of the Bible and no clear convictions on creed or conduct. The old clear-cut lines have become fuzzy. Black and white have been smudged into indefinite gray. Everything is relative, nothing is absolute. There is "no king in Israel" and every man does what is right in his own eyes. "What is right for me may be wrong for you," we hear. An indiscriminate amiability tries to see the good in everything and would have a nice word for the devil himself. Any man with definite judgments on creed and conduct is too angular to fit the smooth, neat patterns of today. Preaching has become tasteless with nothing to chew on, like boneless chicken stewed in cream. Half of what is said cancels the other half and we end up with nothing. The most popular shelf in the homiletic market is in the baby food department. Strong meat is not popular because, as the writer to the Hebrews says, it belongs to the full grown and the discerning.

Nothing is more rare in churches today than discernment. The natural man knows nothing of it, the carnal man is devoid of it. Only the spiritual man has it and we have all too few in that category. To discern the truth, to discern the times, to discern the spirits, to discern the Lord's body, to discern good and evil, here is a field almost unexplored. It is time to get out of the nursery and grow up!

8

The "Foolishness" of God

Nearly twenty centuries ago a weak-eyed missionary preached a sermon on Mars' Hill in Athens. He was not much to look at for it seems his bodily presence wasn't much. Once in a while God produces a good-looking man just to relieve the monotony. It is dangerous for a preacher to be handsome—his profile may raise expectations that his preaching does not justify.

This particular preacher did not make a great impression on this occasion but he was, in fact, the greatest gospel preacher of all time—the apostle Paul. At Athens he stood and preached the gospel in the midst of what

was once the greatest civilization in history. Some of
Paul's sophisticated listeners believed his messages,
some ridiculed him, and others said, "We'll hear you
again sometime." But they never did, for Paul departed
to continue on his missionary journey.

From Athens, Paul went to Corinth where he set a
standard we are in danger of forgetting in these sophisticated times. He wrote: "I determined not to know anything among you, save Jesus Christ, and him crucified"
(1 Cor. 2:2). He declared that the gospel is "the foolishness of God" and "the weakness of God."

We speak of the "wisdom of God" and "God Almighty," but who thinks in terms of the "foolishness"
and "weakness" of God? (1 Cor. 1:25). Paul means that
his message is a contradiction to the wisdom of the
natural man who, he says, is utterly incapable of understanding spiritual truth. Such a man cannot receive the
things of the Spirit of God for they are foolishness to
him; nor can he know them because they are spiritually
discerned. Paul declares that God upsets all our standards by choosing the foolish, the weak, the base, and
the despised; by choosing things that are not to con-
found things that are mighty, that no flesh may glory in
His presence.

Paul's concept of the foolishness and weakness of God
contradicts all modern standards and is so revolutionary
that the church, for the most part, is afraid to try it.
Paul, that unattractive little preacher standing in the
midst of Athens, is a perfect example of the foolishness
and weakness of God versus the wisdom and power of
men. What a contrast and what a confrontation!

Evangelical Christianity is blowing a fuse these days
trying to sound intellectual. We would dress up the foolishness of God in the wisdom of men and fortify the

weakness of God with the power of men. We would modernize religion, revamp worship, and give Jesus a new look. We cheapen the gospel to attract a psychedelic generation. We feel we must be relevant and contemporary, that we must dialogue with the "now," study the spectrum, develop expertise, seek fulfillment in involvement, get down to the nitty-gritty, and so on ad infinitum, ad nauseam. What advantage does a new terminology give us? We used to call it an itch and now it is an allergy but we scratch just the same!

When God sent His Son to this world, He showed scant regard for our culture, philosophy, and intellectualism. There is nothing glamorous about a baby born in a barn to a poor peasant woman (we make the coming of Jesus sound like a fairy tale); there is nothing elegant about a bruised and battered man, His face covered with blood and spittle, dying between two thieves. Even the New Testament Greek is not the classic variety which the Corinthians spoke but rather the language of the marketplace.

Just because the plan of salvation was not worked out by a conference of scholars in a university doesn't mean that there is nothing profound about it. "Great is the mystery of godliness: God was manifest in the flesh, justified in the Spirit, seen of angels, preached unto the Gentiles, believed on in the world, received up into glory" (1 Tim. 3:16). Compared to that, nuclear physics is kindergarten stuff. We shall spend eternity marveling at the wonder of what God has done for us in Christ.

The message of the gospel is so different from anything we would have contrived that the wiseacres and smart alecks of this world call it nonsense, silly, moronic. That is what Paul means by "foolishness" in this passage. The world resents it because it leaves no room for pride and allows no flesh to glory in His presence. They laughed at it in Corinth and they laugh at it today and when we tone it down or dress it up to please this age we waste both our time and theirs for the natural man is not geared to receive it until he has been operated on by the Holy Spirit. God has kept His secrets from the wise and prudent and has revealed them unto babes.

One might as well try to catch sunbeams with a fishhook or discuss nuclear physics with a monument in a city park as to discuss divine revelation with a man of this world. The worldling may be prominent, successful, and a Ph.D. but that gives him no advantage whatever in understanding the things of God.

If the preaching of the cross is to the world foolishness, it follows that preachers of the cross will be to the world fools. Stand in Congress or the UN or any university today and share the gospel and you will be called a moron. This is the foolishness of God. The gospel has never made sense to this world and never will. There are no points of similarity, only points of contrast. It runs against the grain from start to finish. It springs from a different source, runs a different course, and arrives at a different conclusion. We never would have planned it this way.

Paul was not interested in art, culture, and philosophy as he strolled through Athens. What impressed him was, "These people don't know God."

> He had seen the face of Jesus;
> Tell him not of aught beside;
> He had heard the voice of Jesus
> And his soul was satisfied.

So he preached on revelation, resurrection, and repentance. Today we think we must brush up on art appreciation, see the Broadway plays, and sip ginger ale at cocktail parties. We have tried to make the gospel popular but it was never meant for entertainment. When we call in the world, the flesh, and the devil to put Christianity over, we have cheapened it instead of communicating it. We say "The end justifies the means" but the means determines the end.

There is no place for dialogue between the foolishness of God and the wisdom of man. A man without Christ is blind and dead. He cannot see or live until he believes and receives the gospel. Light means nothing to a blind man. He must also have sight.

Long ago a teacher came to Jesus by night. He knew a lot about religion and the Scriptures and had a well-thought-out system but Jesus said to him, "You must be born again." That was new language to Nicodemus. There was no chapter in his book about that. He asked, "How can these things be?" Our Lord answered, in effect, "The trouble is, you have a system and you cannot fit this into your system. You do not add me to what you already have; you need a new system." God does not come to us on *our* terms, we must come to Him on *His* terms. Our Lord is not standing, hat in hand, awaiting our verdict on Him. We are poor sinners awaiting His verdict on us.

In the days of the early church, one might have asked, "What do these Galilean fishermen know about the problems of our time?" But they turned the world upside down with the simple story of a crucified and risen Lord. They did not hold seminars on slavery and symposiums on Caesar. They were "open on the Godward side" and they met the civilization of their day in a head-on collision with "the foolishness of God." Today we are talking over the heads of the common people trying to make Jesus Christ acceptable to highbrows and worldlings. We are talking to people who aren't listening and answering questions nobody is asking.

It has been said that if another revival ever comes it will begin with a persecuted minority, scorning the values of this world and living by stringent discipline. Such men will be "nobodies" in the eyes of this age and fools for the sake of Christ. That is a logical and scriptural conclusion if the answer to our dilemma lies in the foolishness and weakness of God.

9

No More Sea

"And there was no more sea" (Rev. 21:1)

The last book in the Bible was written by a lonely old preacher on a desolate island surrounded by a surging sea. John, the last of the apostles, was in exile on Patmos "for the Word of God and the testimony of Jesus Christ." All the other apostles had died. John might well have asked, "Is this what I get for being a soldier of the cross, a follower of the Lamb?" It looked like persecution but it was really promotion for God pulled back the curtain and revealed the greatest futurama of all time. It was worth exile on Patmos to see that!

The vision reached its climax when John beheld a new heaven and a new earth: "For the first heaven and earth were passed away and there was *no more sea.*" Now why are we given this strange extra information that there was no more sea?

There is a lot of ocean in the Book of Revelation. One hears the roar of the waves all the way through the Apocalypse. One reads about a sea of glass mingled with fire. The star called Wormwood fell on the sea. The beast arose out of the sea. The great angel threw a mighty stone into the sea. When John heard the singing of the multitude of the redeemed it was like the voice of many waters. And when at last he saw the new heaven and the new earth, that sea he was so tired of had disappeared.

Symbol of Mystery

What does it mean? For one thing, the sea is a symbol of mystery. "Thy way is in the sea, and thy path in the great waters, and thy footsteps are not known" (Ps. 77:19); "thy judgments are a great deep" (Ps. 36:6); "O the depth of the riches both of the wisdom and knowledge of God!" (Rom. 11:33). How unsearchable are His judgments and His ways past finding out!

Remember that the Jew was a landlubber, not a seafarer. When he started out from Egypt for the Promised Land, the first thing that got in his way was a sea. There are no seas in Israel (the Sea of Galilee is only a lake). To the Jew, the ocean stood for awesome mystery and awful misery. He preferred green pastures and still waters. And after all the centuries, not only to the Jew but to all the rest of us, the ocean is still not something ordinary and commonplace that we take as a matter of course. In spite of how much we have traveled it, explored it, studied it, or written about it, what a mystery it remains!

What would happen if we could drain it dry? What continents would show up, what canyons and craters, mountains and valleys? Think of the dead that lie in it, the sunken ships entombed in it, the wealth lost in it, the power hidden in it! It is a world of mystery that surrounds us, buried in water.

The sea is a symbol of the mystery we call life. We are so ignorant, we know so little; only a little tip of the iceberg rises above the surface. There are so many knots we cannot untie. When I meet someone who has life's mysteries analyzed and catalogued and correlated, all the i's dotted and all the t's crossed, everything tucked away in convenient cubbyholes, he is not my cup of tea! I still see through a glass darkly and I know only in part. But one day the mystery will clear and there will be no more sea.

Dying itself will answer more riddles and solve more puzzles in five minutes than any man can unravel in a lifetime. When my dear wife changed worlds recently and went to heaven, she suddenly saw more mysteries clear up in an hour than all the philosophers and scholars and experts have discovered in all the centuries. With her and all like her in that land of light there is *no more sea.*

Symbol of Evil

The sea is a symbol of evil. It symbolizes not only mystery but misery. "The wicked are like the troubled

sea . . . whose waters cast up mire and dirt" (Isa. 57:20).
We live in an ocean of evil. Sociologist Arnold Toynbee
pondered long why a nation as literate as Germany
could be deceived by a maniac like Hitler. He concluded
that there must be a vein of original sin in human nature everywhere, that civilization is a thin cake of cus-
tom overlying a molten mass of wickedness that is always boiling up for an opportunity to burst out. Well did
the song writer express it:

> My soul in sad exile was out on life's sea,
> So burdened with sin and distressed. . . .

He went on to say,

> I've anchored my soul in the haven of rest,
> I'll sail the wide seas no more;
> The tempest may sweep o'er the wild, stormy deep—
> In Jesus I'm safe evermore.

The devil stirred up a storm on the Sea of Galilee
while our Lord slept in a boat. He stirred up a tempest
called Euroclydon when Paul was on his voyage toward
Rome. We live on a tempestuous ocean of iniquity but
we look for a new heaven and a new earth wherein
dwells righteousness and where there shall be *no more
sea.*

Symbol of Unrest

"But the wicked are like the troubled sea, when it
cannot rest. . . . There is no peace, saith my God, to the
wicked" (Isa. 57:20–21).

The sea is a symbol of unrest. This world has never

been so restless as it is now. Tranquilizer sales are at a
record high. Mental hospitals are crowded. Drugs, alco-
hol, immorality, broken homes, and broken hearts echo
the words of Isaiah. But God's geography for the new
heaven and new earth does not list any oceans of sin and
unrest. There's a river of life but *no more sea!*

Never has a generation invented so many devices and
spent so much money to make itself comfortable—and
never has there been such an unhappy generation. We
are exiles on Patmos surrounded by a sea of unrest while
men cry "Peace!" when there is no peace.

Symbol of Separation

But more than anything else, the sea is a symbol of
separation. How lonely John must have been on Patmos.
Gone were all the other apostles. Gone was the fellowship of the church and all his Christian friends. No matter which way John looked, there was only that ocean.
How he longed for a day when there would be *no more
sea!*

You and I are exiles on this earth separated from the
saints of centuries past. We can only read about them or
what they wrote. We are also separated from the saints
of our own day who are now with the Lord. I think of
the great preachers I have heard who now are gone. I
think of the dear men and women with whom I have
labored in times past. I feel like the last leaf on the tree
and the wind is blowing hard. I find myself asking, "O
brethren, O sisters, how is it over there?"

I think of personal friends of days past. There was
John Brown back in the days of my first pastorate in the
country. He was a farmer who loved to talk about the

things of God. Many a time we spent much of an afternoon back on the creek just talking when he should have been plowing and I should have been visiting. If the next morning I happened to be back, he never said "Good morning;" we just took up where we had left off the day before. I think one day we'll take off a hundred years of eternity just to catch up!

We think of those dear ones closest to our hearts. My old father used to meet me at the little railroad station when I came home from my preaching trips. He always had one question to begin with: "How did you get along?" I suspect he will ask that same question when there is no more sea and our separation is ended.

Not long ago the dearest of all went across that sea of separation. A few weeks later I was preaching in St. Augustine, Florida. I was staying at a motel facing the waterfront. Early each morning I walked the full length of the promenade and looked across to the whitecaps breaking along the distant beach. How I longed for the touch of a vanished hand and the sound of a voice that was still. My heart called, "Darling, how is it over there? All I can see is the ocean. God hasten the day when there will be *no more sea!*"

That day is coming! William Jennings Bryan said, "Life is a narrow strip between the companionship of yesterday and the reunion of tomorrow." Best of all, better than reunion with earth's dear ones is the prospect of seeing Him whom, though now we see Him not, we love.

When my life-work is ended and I cross the swelling tide,
When the bright and glorious morning I shall see,
I shall know my Redeemer when I reach the other side,
And His smile will be the first to welcome me.

I don't like tears but God will wipe all tears from my eyes. I don't like darkness but there will be no night there. I don't like clouds but that will be the land of unclouded day. I don't like pain but neither shall there be any more pain. I don't like death but nobody dies there. I don't like sorrow but over there we do not weep. I don't like separation but there will be *no more sea.* We are exiles on Patmos but we are not here to stay.

The more the church drives down her tent pegs in this world and lives at ease down here, the less she cares for the Book of Revelation. But when the tempests shake the curtains of this temporary dwelling place, the more does she value this precious little book John wrote on Patmos. Laodicean Christians, "rich and increased with goods (and needing) nothing" (Rev. 3:17), with loved ones still around them and earthly circumstances in good shape, do not read the Apocalypse. But when evil days come and we find no pleasure in them, we treasure the Patmos futurama.

We are not cast down (Ps. 42:5) as we behold America and the whole world entering what may be a time of great trouble. We are not shaking our heads. Rather, we lift them up for our redemption draws nigh and we are looking forward to a new heaven and a new earth, the blessed "Land of No More"—no more death, no more sorrow, no more crying, no more tears, no more pain, no more curse, no more night.

And, thank God, *no more sea!*

10

No Prophet in Bethel

Bethel, like many other places and people in the Bible, is a sad example of a glorious beginning followed by a tragic finish. It was at Bethel that Jacob's hard pillow of stone became a holy pillar of dedication, and it was to Bethel he returned after backsliding. The day came when Jeroboam II set up a golden calf in Bethel, but like the golden calf in the wilderness, it brought down the wrath of God. When the prophet Amos thundered against idolatry and corruption, he uttered in holy sarcasm, "Come to Bethel, and transgress; at Gilgal, multiply transgression." Bethel was the political, social, and religious capital of apostate Israel. It had a court preacher, Amaziah, who was horrified at the countryfied ministry of Amos and bade him return from the boulevards to the backwoods.

Our modern "Bethel" has its easy religion and golden calves and court chaplains but no prophet stands today in the royal court. False prophets abound but nothing faintly resembling Amos has appeared on the scene of late. There is no Nathan who will reprove David. There is no Elijah who will confront Ahab. No Micaiah faces two kings headed for Ramoth-gilead, telling it like it is. No Jehu asks Jehoshaphat, "Shouldest thou help the ungodly and love them that hate the Lord?" No John the Baptist reproves a king for adultery. No Paul today preaches righteousness, temperance, and judgment to come until Felix trembles (Acts 24:25). No Savonarola dares the wrath of the Medicis. No Luther bucks the Establishment of his time while smooth Erasmus trims down "No" until it sounds like "Yes." There is no successor to John Knox, a man feared more by Queen Mary than all the armies of her enemies.

The should-be prophet of today, given an invitation to Bethel, is more likely to spend his time complimenting his host and dispensing pleasant generalities. Worse than blind leaders of the blind are bland leaders of the bland. They offer plausible arguments for their policies, not reasons but excuses (which are only skins of reasons stuffed with lies).

The atmosphere of these times is not conducive to prophetic preaching. Pastors, teachers, and evangelists are plentiful and God be thanked for all of them but there is also a place in the divine economy and the New Testament gifts for the prophet. Pastors, teachers, and evangelists may on occasion preach prophetic sermons but we

are thinking now of full-time prophets, not foretellers
but forth-tellers who speak for God to the nation and the
church. Bethel is ripe for such a ministry but candidates
for that ministry are few and far between. It is utterly
impossible to be a popular prophet. No preacher in history ever achieved that.

The next prophet in Bethel will not come from the
wise, mighty, and noble, the intelligentsia and the VIPs.
Amos declared that he was not a prophet by profession
("I was no prophet"), nor by parentage ("Neither was I a
prophet's son"), but by providence ("And the Lord took
me as I followed the flock"). Those are sufficient creden-
tials today as then! No cautious pulpit politician would
dream of facing Bethel with such equipment. It takes a
certain breed to produce a "Troubler from Tekoah" as
Amos was.

It is significant that when a nation that started out
rugged becomes rich and then rotten, along with this
moral deterioration comes a corresponding tolerance
and acceptance on the part of its spiritual leaders. When
Ahab and Jehoshaphat decided to go up against Ramoth-
gilead, four hundred prophets got on the bandwagon. We
are plainly told in the Scriptures that in the last days
men will not endure sound doctrine and will depart
from the truth and heap to themselves teachers to tickle
their itching ears. We live in an epidemic of this itch
and popular preachers have developed ear-tickling into
an art.

Today the new angle is to avoid all "negative" preaching and accentuate only the positive. Some preachers
say they never condemn sin in their preaching except
when it shows up in the Scripture they may be expound-
ing. Fortunately it shows up pretty often in the New
Testament; otherwise, most congregations would never

hear of it! The American Bethel needs an Amos. He must needs be sold out to the Almighty, shipwrecked on God, and stranded on Omnipotence. He may be called from a pursuit as lowly as figs and flocks. His worst opposition will come from the clergy. He will be called a negative preacher.

There was another prophet who visited Bethel and his sad experience warns us to this day. God commanded him to deliver his message and depart immediately, lingering with no one. He declined the invitation of King Jeroboam to stay awhile and if he had gone home from there he would be considered a great prophet. But instead we do not even know his name because he succumbed to the invitation of another prophet and a lion slew him. Alexander Whyte wrote a masterpiece about this singular character and the refrain that underlies it is "Alas, my brother!" This prophet was tired, had been under quite a strain and failed to beware of somebody who claimed to have heard from God. This is always dangerous business—unwise sociability has been the undoing of many a prophet. Fraternizing with apostates is a peril common to Jeroboam's day and our own.

There is no evidence that Amos was awed by any of the grandeur he saw in Bethel. Dr. Kyle Yates wrote: "His time had not been spent in a divinity school. He was unwilling to be classed as a member of the guilds who made a living by bowing to the wishes of the people and preaching a pleasing message that would guarantee a return engagement."

Amos was not looking for a return invitation. He had not been invited there in the first place!

11

Coming to See Jesus

One of the strange developments of these weird times is the amazing popularity of the name "Jesus." The musical, *Jesus Christ, Superstar,* swept the country; we had the Jesus Movement, Jesus People, and the Jesus Generation. Of course there has been a true "Jesus Movement" ever since our Lord came to earth, and wherever men trust and follow Him you have "Jesus people." But today the name above every name has been dragged in the slime, mixed with demonic drumbeats, and cheapened and prostituted to the level of this pagan age. A coarse and crude familiarity slaps God on the back and despises the church while a bearded and barefoot generation is out looking for "the real Jesus."

The twelfth chapter of John's Gospel tells us about some Greeks who came to see Jesus one day (vv. 20–21). It was a day of crisis in the life of our Lord. He had recently raised Lazarus from the dead and everybody was talking about it; many believed on Him because of it (11:45). On this day, at the peak of his fame and popularity, Jesus had made His triumphal entry into Jerusalem.

But if He was at the height of His popularity, He was also at the height of His opposition. His enemies were planning to do away with Him. Things were coming to a head and the storm was about to break, the inevitable collision between Christ and antichrist. Against this background and at this moment these Greeks came, asking to see Jesus. Maybe they had come to invite Him to Athens! What if He had decided to be a world teacher in Athens and Alexandria and Rome? What if He had given in to the temptation to be an earthly Messiah?

When Philip and Andrew took news of the visitors' request to Jesus, He did not respond as we might expect. He gave an enigmatic answer: "The hour is come that the Son of man should be glorified" (John 12:23). Mind you, He did not say "crucified" but "glorified." How could He be glorified by dying a criminal's death? He explained it: "Verily, verily, I say unto you, Except a corn of wheat fall into the ground and die, it abideth alone: but if it die, it bringeth forth much fruit" (vs. 24). He is saying, "If I remained only a teacher I could never atone for the sin of the world. As Son of God and Son of man, I must identify myself with sinful humanity, gather up in me the whole race of Adam, and take it to the grave with me. As the wheat dies and comes up again in many grains of wheat, so I must rise again bringing with me a whole new race, risen to walk in newness of life. I am facing death and resurrection and if you do not see me in that light, you do not see me at all."

Too many "Greeks" looking for Jesus today are not looking for a crucified Savior and risen Lord. They are looking for Jesus the radical or Jesus the revolutionary. Some are seeking a religious substitute for the thrills they sought in drugs or sex. They need to take a look at this momentous occasion in the life of Christ and then face the real issue.

On this day of crisis Jesus said, "The hour is come" (vs. 23). All His life he had anticipated that hour. He had said to His mother at Cana, "Mine hour is not yet come." When men sought to lay hands on Him they could not "because His hour was not yet come." But now His hour *had* come and it was to be the greatest hour in history when God would fight it out with the devil and settle the sin question forever.

Jesus said further, "Now is my soul troubled; and what shall I say? Father, save me from this hour: but for this cause came I unto this hour" (v. 27). John does not record the Gethsemane experience but this provides a foretaste. Some have asked why Jesus seemed to shrink from the cross when another man, Socrates, drank hemlock without flinching. But Socrates was not dying for the sins of the world. Jesus being who He is and sin being what it is, this death took all evil—past, present, and future—and nailed it to the cross. No wonder He said, "Now is my soul troubled."

He also prayed, "Father, glorify Thy name" (v. 28). Incidentally, that suggests that when our souls are troubled and we know not what to say, we should pray as Jesus did, "Father, glorify Thy name." The supreme purpose of Jesus' life was to glorify God. It is our main business too and it is the chief end of prayer. Dr. R. A. Torrey said, "The purpose of prayer is that God may be glorified in the answer." In answer to our Lord's prayer a voice from heaven said, "I have both glorified it and will glorify it again."

Jesus had already said, "The hour is come." At His arrest in the garden He said, "This is *your hour*, and the power of darkness" (Luke 22:53). It was *His* hour for which He had come into the world but it was also *their* hour when the opposition of the devil reached its climax, when light met darkness and heaven met hell. Here was the climax, the "death grapple in the darkness twixt old systems and the Word." It was *His* hour. It was *their* hour.

Jesus announced the arrival of this hour, this climax, this conflict, by stating: "Now is the judgment of this world: now shall the prince of this world be cast out. And I, if I be lifted up from the earth, will draw all men unto me" (vv. 31–32). The world had been under the judgment of God ever since man had fallen into sin. Now all who would accept the provision God was making in the death of His Son would belong to a new race, while all who did not would remain under judgment. ("He that believeth on him is not condemned: but he that believeth not is condemned already, because he hath not believed in the name of the only begotten Son of God.")

It was on the day of this great announcement that the Greeks came to see Jesus. Our Lord was not excited by the appearance of these potential Greek converts. Indeed the grain of wheat must die and rise again before Gentiles could be received. The Jesus that many modern "Greeks" are looking for is not this Christ. They have

invented an imaginary Jesus and the cross is only a
charm to wear around the neck. These people say they
are not interested in doctrine and they are disgusted
with the church. They are out looking for the "real"
Jesus but He is not hard to find; He is looking for them.
The problem is that men do not like to face sin and its
cure—the cross—and they dodge the resurrection just
as *Jesus Christ, Superstar* did.

Our Lord was not speaking only of His own death and
resurrection that day. He also announced that "He that
loveth his life shall lose it, and he that hateth his life in
this world shall keep it unto life eternal" (v. 25). If we
are to follow Him we must be willing to be His seed-
corn, to be planted in the plot of His choosing. This, of
course, means death to self. But most modern "Greeks"
are not interested in being grain-of-wheat Christians.
This is a day of escapism. Life is too much for us and we
try to dodge it in a hundred ways.

It's nice to visit Disneyland but we cannot live there.
The Christian life is not a vacation but a vocation, not
a picnic but a pilgrimage. Its mountain-top experiences
can flatten out and drop from the majestic to the mo-
notonous and even to the miserable. Even our Lord
said, "Now is my soul troubled." Paul did not spend
his last days writing his memoirs on the sunny Riviera.
If you can believe tradition, all the disciples but one
died violent deaths. The roll call of faith heroes in Hebrews lists many who subdued kingdoms, wrought righteousness, obtained promises, stopped the mouths of
lions, quenched the violence of fire, escaped the edge of
the sword, and otherwise were eminently successful;
but it lists another category ("and others") who died in
adversity.

There is much going on among young people today

that is encouraging. I am having a better response from youth than at any time in my ministry. Many are seeking a fresh and original experience of Jesus Christ. But young people, like all the rest of us, can be deceived and Satan is the master deceiver. The devil is not fighting religion. He is too smart for that. He is producing a counterfeit Christianity so much like the real one that good Christians are afraid to speak out against it.

Some are saying of this movement and that, "If it is a fad, at least it is a religious fad and so I'm for it." But if it is a fad, it is false and it is a fearful thing to be tricked into a false religious experience. Better none at all! We welcome all young "Greeks" who have come to see Jesus but they need Philips and Andrews to lead them to the true Christ for many false Christs abound in these last days—exactly as our Lord said they would.

All young "Greeks" who say they are interested in Jesus need to face the Christ of John 12. They need to hear His call to rigid discipline, self-denial, and the straight and narrow way. They must take up their cross and follow Him who came not to send peace but a sword.

How many young "Greeks" are willing to be seed-corn Christians, dying to self and multiplying in lives won to the Savior? Many are willing to be recluse saints in some utopian commune or dream Shangri-la, but who is willing to be the salt of the earth rubbed daily into the carcass of humanity? We need no more fastidious church members who are willing to minister to human need only after it has been deodorized and disinfected.

A display of garden seeds in pretty packages is a lovely sight but no food will be furnished for the table until the packages have been torn open and the seeds have been planted in the dirty old earth. Alas, there is too much *packaged* Christianity and not enough *planted* Christianity! Who is willing to say,

> Come ill, come well, the cross, the crown,
> The rainbow or the thunder;
> I fling my soul and body down
> For God to plow them under.

Who is willing to sing:

> I take, O cross, thy shadow
> For my abiding place;
> I ask no other sunshine
> Than the sunshine of His face;
> Content to let the world go by
> To know no gain nor loss,
> My sinful self my only shame,
> My glory all the cross.

Shadow and sunshine! Jesus for the joy set before Him endured the cross, despising the shame. He reached the sunshine through the shadow. Who follows in His train?

12

"Why?"

One of the words most often on the lips of children is that never-ending query, "Why?" Every parent lives under a steady barrage of "Why, why, why?" From childhood on we question the Almighty, "Why did this have to happen to me?" We see the trouble and tragedy, the misery and the mystery, the iniquities and the inequities of life—so much that does not add up or make sense.

Job cried, "Oh that I knew where I might find him!. . . Behold, I go forward, but he is not there; and backward, but I cannot perceive him: On the left hand, where he doth work, but I cannot behold him: he hideth himself on the right hand, that I cannot see him" (Job 23:3, 8–9). David lamented, "O God, why hast thou cast us off forever? why doth thine anger smoke against the sheep of thy pasture?" (Ps. 74:1). Jeremiah moaned, "Why is my pain perpetual, and my wound incurable, which refuseth to be healed? wilt thou be altogether unto me as a liar, and as waters that fail?" (Jer. 15:18).

We make our way through a maze of unanswered questions, through mysteries with no possible solutions—that is, until we have better light. Everything is mixed: one day may see a precious answer to prayer, the next may witness some strange calamity. One day brings miracle and the next brings misery and it adds up to mystery. It is like the weather with sunny skies and singing birds followed by hurricane and destruction; there is no discernible pattern because even the weather was fouled up by the fall of man.

So one day of green pastures and still waters is followed by dark valleys and miry swamps and a thousand "whys" lie unanswered, tabled for future reference. If you have walked through a hospital for crippled or retarded children; if you have visited cemeteries where lie countless soldiers who died in vain; if you have looked at the victims of tornado, fire, and flood or the corpses of innocent men and women murdered by demoniacs; if you have observed the haunting faces of alcoholics and drug addicts or have held the hand of a dying loved one; if you have faced ironic enigmas that add up to nothing in your arithmetic; if dreams have been blasted and hope destroyed by a heartless law of cause and effect, your heart must cry out to God with the biggest little word in your vocabulary, "Why?"

I think of a year that started out so pleasantly for my

beloved and me. We had made plans for delightful months ahead together. Instead, I sat by her bedside and watched her die of an unusual disease. She expected to be healed but she died. Now, all hopes of a happy old age together are dashed to the ground. I plod alone with the other half of my life on the other side of death. My hand reaches for another hand now vanished and I listen at night for the sound of a voice that is still. And I am tempted a thousand times to ask, "My God, why . . .?"

God is patient with our complaints. He knows our frame and remembers that we are dust. But we do not need to bombard heaven with our unanswered questions because He has gathered up all our agony and distress and answered all our "whys" in one all-inclusive "Why?" We cannot fathom the depths of that "Why?" but we can rest in the certainty that in it is found the reason for all our sorrow, the key to all our troubles, and the fulfillment of every shattered dream.

It began with David and the Twenty-second Psalm. Centuries before Jesus died on the cross David put into writing a description of the crucifixion. When you remember that crucifixion was a Roman and not a Jewish form of execution, only divine inspiration can account for a man writing hundreds of years in advance a word picture of Calvary. He describes the bones out of joint, the agony, the thirst, the pierced hands and feet, the scornful onlookers, the casting of lots—all were precisely fulfilled when the Savior died. And our Lord climaxed His suffering by uttering the very words with which David began, "My God, my God, why hast thou forsaken me?"

What does it mean? When Luther studied this passage he sat motionless for hours and rose at last to say, "God forsaken of God! Who can understand it?"

That is exactly what happened. For a brief moment a
holy God who cannot look on sin turned His back while
His son drank the dregs of that cup, when sin was dealt
with once for all, that God might be just and the Justi-
fier, that the judgment seat might become the mercy
seat, that God might be propitiated and men reconciled.
All our heartaches and troubles and unanswered "whys"
grow out of the fact that this world was wrecked by sin.
But God started a new race of man and undertook its
redemption—a redemption that will be climaxed when
Christ returns to set up His kingdom.

After my Lord cried "My God, why?" He said, "It is
finished." And finished it was, but it awaits final fulfillment. We see not yet all things put under Him but we
see Jesus. I do not need to ask "My God, why?" because
all my "whys" were taken care of in the only recorded
time that Jesus ever asked "Why?" He asked it that I
may never need to ask it. He was forsaken that I may
never be forsaken, forsaken for *one* moment that I may
never be forsaken *any* moment! It assures me of the
ultimate destruction of the devil and a day when my
fears will vanish, my tears will be dried, and what I lost
temporarily I will gain eternally.

So at the very time when I have more unanswered
questions than ever, I have never been more certain that
all things are working together for good. Although truth
may seem forever on the scaffold and wrong forever on
the throne, God stands within the shadows keeping
watch above His own.

It is ridiculous to arrive at final conclusions before we
reach the end of the book. When a new building is going
up there is always much rubbish. Broken pieces and left-
overs clutter the scene. But when the building is completed, the trash is carted away and the new edifice

stands clean and complete. God's construction job is not finished and we grow weary with broken fragments that do not fit the blueprint. But we have not seen the end of it and He who has begun a good work in us is pledged to complete it and dispose of all the rubbish.

As a little boy I enjoyed watching my mother make bread or cake. When she assembled the ingredients, they did not look too appetizing. Who wants to eat flour or baking powder? But when she had mixed everything in proper proportions and put them in the oven we awaited the outcome with joy. Sometimes the happenings in our lives are not enjoyable when they come separately one by one. But when God has completed the recipe and put it through the baking, we have "Romans 8:28 cake" and the taste is good, even though some of the ingredients at one time made us weep.

You may be a theologian or wish to understand the *how* of something, but you need never ask "Why?" because Calvary covers it all. When before the throne we stand in Him complete, all the riddles that puzzle us here will fall into place and we shall *know* in fulfillment what we now *believe* in faith—that all things worked together for good in His eternal purpose. No longer will we cry "My God, why?" Instead, "alas" will become "Alleluia," all question marks will be straightened into exclamation points, sorrow will change to singing, and pain will be lost in praise.